BLACK MEN STILL SINGING

poems by
Maurice W. Britts
Alberto O. Cappas
George D. Clabon
Bernard V. Finney, Jr.
William Goodin
Albert McClure
Gary Smith
Chema Ude
Ken Wibecan
Gene A. Williams

GUILD PRESS

P.O. Box 22583
Robbinsdale, MN
55422

International Standard Book Number 0-940248-38-7
Library Of Congress Catalog Card Number 90-80971
Copyright © 1990 Guild Press
SECOND PRINTING 1994

ALL RIGHTS RESERVED
Reproduction in whole or in part without written permission is prohibited,
except by a reviewer who may quote brief passages in a review.

CONTENTS

MAURICE W. BRITTS .... 1 - 6
"My Hope For The Future," "The Color Of My Skin," "Why Do I Love You," "The House Is Empty Now," "Used," "Keep That Nigger Runnin'," "Fooling Ourselves," "The Hardest Thing," "When The Earth Yawns," "What Do You Do With A Wasted Life"

ALBERTO O. CAPPAS .... 7 - 12
"Collaboration," "Distant Despair," "Doña Julia," "Her Boricua," "Yuppie's Love Poem," "The Ruse," "Stickball"

GEORGE D. CLABON .... 13 - 18
"B Flat Scale," "Reflections" "Future Consideration," "What Price," "Stolen Treasure," "Highpockets," "Storyteller," "Dibs/No Dibs," "Conversation"

BERNARD V. FINNEY, JR. .... 19 - 24
"I Believe," "Expectation," "Black Legacy," "Frozen In The Snow," "Ten Thousand Spiderwebs," "The Sky Blinks," "Angry," "The Plague (Aids)," "A Summer's Awakening," "The Night," "Protect Me," "Tomorrow Is Out To Sea"

WILLIAM GOODIN .... 25 - 30
"I Dream Of Many Things," "In The Confines Of His Home," "Within My Life," "With You," "One Nation Under God," "Looking In The Mirror," "Forgive Me For Crying But I Can't Help It"

ALBERT McCLURE .... 31 - 36
"Why Do I Weep?," "The Wind Of Death," "The She-Hunters Of The Deep Forest," "Old People," "Africa," "Values," "A Part Of Living," "Fascinating," "Nothingness Of Silence"

GARY SMITH .... 37 - 42
"Secondhand Radio," "Mose Goodman," "Winters In Holly Springs," "Slavery Made You A Poet," "Your Poem To Phyllis," "Unfinished Errands," "The Winter Of Your Death," "The Fate Of An Innocent Dog," "Flannel Suit"

CHEMA UDE .... 43 - 48
"Saved Africa," "A Capital Prayer," "African Patricidal Plot," "Hidebound," "My Nigerian Freedom," "Nature's Way," "The One I Chose," "Our African Parents," "Manhood Rights"

KEN WIBECAN .... 49 - 54
"Black History," "To Black Woman," "Earthbound," "Harold," "Return Engagement," "Adventure," "Why Dogs Bark At Night," "Photograph Of A 1923 Lynching"

GENE A. WILLIAMS (Sunji Ali) .... 55 - 60
"Poetry In The Alley," "The Blues Is Sweet Water," "Walking On The Water," "Hazel Eyes," "Mother Didn't Tell Me To Cry," "Rising To The Moment"

INTRODUCTION

Dr. Maurice W. Britts
Alberto O. Cappas
George D. Clabon
Bernard V. Finney, Jr.
William Goodin

Albert McClure
Dr. Gary Smith
Chema Ude
Ken Wibecan
Gene A. Williams

We keep hearing in the mass media that Black men are, at worst, an endangered species or, at best, merely irrelevant.

But we in Guild Press believe — "It ain't so!" And we hope that people who hear or read the poems in *BLACK MEN STILL SINGING* — whether the poems be the blues, gospel or love songs — will also know: "Here are some real men — Black men with pride, insight, skill and power."

For these poets are part of the people Margaret Walker prophesied in the last few lines of her famous 1937 poem "For My People":

". . . Let a second generation full of courage issue forth, let a people loving freedom come to growth, let a beauty full of healing and a strength of final clenching be the pulsing in our spirits and our blood. Let the martial songs be written, let the dirges disappear. Let a race of men now rise and take control."

Leon Knight
Senior Editor

Dr. Maurice W. Britts

grew up near Alton, Illinois, and has lived in Minnesota for the past 38 years. He received his doctorate from the University of Minnesota and is a retired public school administrator.

The father of nine (including eight who have earned college degrees), Dr. Britts teaches African-American literature for Metropolitan State University, Minneapolis. He has authored four books — scholarly, popular history and poetry — and edited three books of poetry.

MY HOPE FOR THE FUTURE

I want to open my eyes and ears
To enjoy the music that one hears
After the rain has scrubbed the hills
And filled the air with scented thrills.
I want to see the rising sun,
To see it when its course is run.
I want to discover each hidden nook
That's nestled near the winding brook.
For once my prospect looked dark and bleak
And I was very beat and weak.
The strength with which I started life
Had ebbed away through daily strife;
But love for what I want to do
Cheered me and came shining through
The cloudy mist of bitter days
That shrouded life with daily haze.
Now renewed I sing my song
And feel way deep inside that long
After snow has left the pines
Folks will be content to sing my lines.

THE COLOR OF MY SKIN

I cried a tear
        Long ago —
The future seemed so bleak.
My mother said,
        "Cheer up, my child,
The future's yours to make.
        Don't let that future
Be the color of your skin."

I think back now
        To those words
And know how right she was.
I rededicate myself
To throwing off those shackles.
Still — Why can't I forget
        The color of my skin?

WHY DO I LOVE YOU?

I love you for the sparkles
Of joy and sadness in your eyes.
I love you for the warm smile
That lingers a tender while
On the cheeks of your dimpled face.
I love you for your fond embrace;
Gentle smile; half-play caress;
The silver softness in your voice.
I love you because you see
My faults and keep on loving me.

THE HOUSE IS EMPTY NOW

The house is empty now.
We've sorted, packed, discarded
      sixty years and more
of life and love saved
      and lost.
Little momentoes—
      my brother's graduation pin
      the battered scout-canteen
      my high school football letter
      Dad's military discharge
He died some thirty years before
and, yet, you held on.
      Your wedding dress
How lovely you must have looked!

The house is empty now,
      empty of the glad times,
      sad times, steely fight times.
All is over for you now.

When the house was full,
I learned
      sharing, caring
      strength of will
            from you.
You fought for me
      a lifetime.
Pride, love, respect
instilled in me
      meant life
as I danced across the world,
      away from the house
           and you,
the house that's empty now.

USED

When you're young
        hope glows bright.
You are challenged
with   dreams and schemes
        to find a place
        among the stars,
called to outstrip the past,
        leave slavery's chains
            behind.

Now older,
        suddenly you see
a place among the stars
was never meant to be.
        Black leaders are used
        to keep others
        from shooting stars —
            including me.

KEEP THAT NIGGER RUNNIN'

Once   a long time ago
I thought —
        The world 's a rosy place
        full of fireworks,
        love and happiness,
        all of it just for me.
Rockets in the sky
raining bright laughter down
        on me,
kissing my cheeks
with feathery touches of love
and soft whispers —
"Tomorrow is even better."

        That was eons ago —
sky rockets never flew.
The night remained dark
with the repetitive refrain —
        "Keep that Nigger runnin'!"

FOOLING OURSELVES

We don't agree on things
        We never did.
We made accommodations
        Focused on little things
That caused conflict
        Evoked rage in each other.

We don't agree on things
        We never did.
We closed our eyes
        Rosied up the passing years
Fooled ourselves
        Falsely thinking
Our lives were like all lives.

We don't agree on things
        We never did.
And with the fading years
        We came to believe
Some little precious moments
        Larger than life
Gave the illusion of agreement.

THE HARDEST THING

The hardest thing in the world
is   to step out   of oneself,
to laugh at the prisoner
        in the shell.

I know a woman who says
        she can do just that.
Observed her one time
as   she   stretched
      and   strained,
finally making it
        on the outside
                of self,
only to see herself
                as herself,
not as others see her.

WHEN THE EARTH YAWNS

The open grave
      stood silent
in the garden of stone,
waiting patiently
      its precious load,
beckoning me.
"Come — enhance my garden,
      rest among the giants
            nestled here."

The earth yawned.
"I am your prize.
      I am all
      you have won.
This garden
      has   no blacks
            no whites,
just completed journeys
      with terminated hope."

WHAT DO YOU DO WITH A WASTED LIFE

What do you do with a wasted life
When your dreams are spent
And there is nothing ahead
Of the good times you once knew?

What do you do with a wasted life
When you've tried and tried
And all you see is failure ahead
And the bubble has burst for you?

What do you do with a wasted life
When you're breathing and moving
Stepping toward the depths of tomorrow
After a day of shattered pain?

What do you do with a wasted life?
Revamp; reconsider; turn around —
Struggle to your feet for one more fight
Find some dream and hold on tight.

Alberto O. Cappas

the father of "two beautiful daughters," graduated from Harlem Prep School and earned a joint degree in American and Black Studies, with a concentration in Puerto Rican Literature and Sociology, from SUNY/Buffalo. He currently lives in New York City where he is employed with the New York State Division for Youth.

Through his writing, Alberto tries "to capture the struggle for survival and recognition that has become synonymous with being a Puerto Rican in the United States."

COLLABORATION

Art,
music,
culture,
    a bomb falls upon society.
Joy,
laughter,
tears,
    a bomb falls upon society.
Artist,
actor,
musician,
    a bomb falls upon society.
Wealth,
fame,
poverty,
    a bomb falls upon society.
Ambition,
success,
failure,
    a bomb falls upon society.
Politics,
religion,
followers,
    a poem can spread destruction
    racing
    through the city
    on the side of a
        subway car.

DISTANT DESPAIR

Up the corner building,
West 105th Street,
woman and her three children
are evicted for not paying the rent.

Down the block, children play
army, moving on to strategic
backyard war games.

Mrs. Garcia, glued to the window,
looking for stories to talk about.

Little Jose, sleeping in the room
next to the window of the adjacent building,
caught a roach preparing to make
a trip into his right ear.

Willie hates cold water, but
takes cold bath under useless protest.

Coño man.

Tia Juanita, recuperating from,
a ghetto breakdown, came home
from the hospital, new ancient ceiling
came down and opened up
her big ugly head.

Coming from Long Island,
      doing ninety with sixty nine volkswagon,
big damn smile and all,
      the landlord
      intends
      to collect his rent.

DOÑA JULIA

Doña Julia committed suicide last night
    cause the welfare department demanded
    too many documents she didn't know existed.
Her utilities were removed.
    The landlord proudly gave her eviction papers.
    The friendly Bodega accused her of trespassing.
Holding on to hope,
    Doña Julia visited Puerto Rican leaders, with fancy titles,
    who promised things that never arrived.
Doña Julia always made it a point to vote
    with the democrats.
    The party of the poor she used to say.

Doña Julia committed suicide last night
    cause life was angry with her, she told her spirits.
And the people that didn't know her, with fancy titles,
always found things to say about her.

Her daughter Evelyn disappeared with this dude,
    Hector, who promised her everything he didn't have.
And her son Jose dropped out of school at ten
    took her money to pay his expenses
    and other things for the dead head
    disappeared looking for his fellows
    who were never around
    when he didn't have anything.

Doña Julia committed suicide
    cause life was angry with her.
Her dead face had a smile
police officers didn't understand.
Someone who couldn't read
found a note and flushed it down the toilet
thinking it had something to do with numbers.
The note said something about one way
    or the other,
"I'm going back to my own country."

HER BORICUA

Doña Rivera,
>the one everybody comes to when
>they run into unresolved situations,

was sold the moon yesterday.
She was very happy cause the
salesman gave her a break,
>telling her she did not have
>to pay taxes on it.

It was tax free,
>he told her.

All her neighbors were surprised
that she accomplished such a big thing.
So they assembled and celebrated
her new fortune.

They decided that Doña Rivera should
keep it a secret or else
the welfare department would
take the moon away from her

Time passed and Doña Rivera became
a very proud woman.
At night, especially when the moon was
in full circle, Doña Rivera would
stay up late and admire the beauty of
>her new possession.

On weekend nights,
she would invite her relatives
>and best friends

over to share the experience with them.

See,
she would tell her relatives and friends,
>in this country
>>you have the freedom to buy
>>>anything you want.

YUPPIE'S LOVE POEM
(for the street people)

This is a love poem for all the
    street people
looking for me to give them a dime,
    a quarter,
    a dollar.
Anything that would help them get closer
    to a bite to eat, a drink
    or to get high,
This is a love poem for all the
    street people

The wise ones   old ones
welfare ones   retarded ones
normal ones   lazy ones
slick ones   the   fuckedup ones
and those that are getting ready
to become street people
    in the future.

This is a love poem for all the
    street people
looking at me with disappointment
when I keep passing them by
    without acknowledging their presence.
Jesuscrist, give me a break
let me pass those street corners
without running into your hands.
    I have rent to pay.
    Installment payments to catch up to,
    Mastercard, Visa and American
    Express to maintain.
Give me a break.
    What obligations do you have?
    Anyway things will get better
Just have some faith.
I do.

THE RUSE

Take your tropical self
into the avenues
    of Arbor Hill
and observe
the disappointed bodies
    mourning
    those who went.
Stonewalls and Rockefeller,
signs of things kept secret.
    You sing
    in the cold winter
and all the politicians
will buy a ticket
to your annual fundraiser.
    Be polite,
do not wear polyester suits,
stay away from cuchifritos
drink martinis,
and   speak English
without broken-down clues.

STICKBALL

Summer screams,
where halfnaked bodies dance
    in the shadow   of the gringo sun,
where streets become playgrounds
and fire hydrants become beaches,
and rooftops a place to get closer
    to the sun.
Catching other illusions,
watching Joselito playing   cowboys and Indians,
and Eddie in the corner
talking about the Viceroys against the Sinners,
and Angel and Junior inventing
a baseball field in the backyard,
and Bobby, the junkie,   committing a robbery,
his solution to the problem,
and Carmen under the stairs with Pete,
    losing innocence,
and Juan, playing stickball in the middle
of the street, got killed by a gringo
driver who didn't understand recreation
on this side of town.

George D. Clabon

was born in St. Louis and moved to Northfield, Minnesota, to attend Carleton College. After completimg his degree, he settled in Minneapolis where he is a supervisor for Prudential Insurance.

His writing is based on his life experience as a Black American and on his view of the world. And about his writing, he hopes that "my poetry will serve as words of guidance/lessons for future generations."

B FLAT SCALE

Relaxation
came easier as a child

I'd sit on the back porch
    on the wooden rail
      at a ninety degree angle
and play my sax

I loved the sensuous/sexy sound
    of the tenor
but I played the alto
    it was lighter to carry when marching

On those sunny/cloudy days
    in St Louis
I wondered
    would I ever leave the shadows
    of those streets
    where crime and poverty
    lived along with
      family love

I ran a B flat scale
to clear my mind
    relaxation . . .

REFLECTIONS

I sat on the bedside
listening to KMOJ
reading the words I had just written
trying to envision
      your reaction
would they be received
as intended
or viewed in another light

I felt my body swaying
to the rhythm of Grace
      pulling up to the bumper
I extended my hand
      within my mind
and said hello

The need to clarify
      left me

FUTURE CONSIDERATION

Fortune or fame
I ask not from my writings

of how we try to outrun
the headless horseman
in a battle with technology
      for souls

or of how we persist
in creating divisions
among humans
      classified like zoo animals
        forbidden to leave our cages
while we pump pollutants
into the arteries of our foundation

I only wish to preserve
the follies of the time
I have shared on this globe
      with others
for future consideration

WHAT PRICE

What price for success
Are you willing to pay
Asked the wizened sage
Ebony face creased by years
Of lifes experiences
And the young man
Looked deeply into his eyes
And saw the vision

> Money
> Is the root of evil
> Said the preacher man
> And the congregation said
> Amen

He rested in the depths
Of frustration
As values/ideals he held
Were shattered
In his quest for the dream
And part of himself
He left behind
As he strove for the star
Of success

> I said
> Money
> Is the root of evil
> And the flock said
> Amen

STOLEN TREASURE

We created the perfect camouflage
Protecting us from discovery
While we stole their greatest treasure
Given to them by the God of our fathers

We colored the world in black and white
And in the confusion
Escaped with their humanity

HIGHPOCKETS

over in front
of Pearl's beauty saloon
three young men
gathered to play
      guitars
changing the parts
      bass, rhythm, lead
      as they talked
of future travels together
      as minstrels
while the proprietor
prepared
      ribs, chicken, snouts
      for public
      consumption

i watched him as he consumed
      more drinks
      his eyes sad
      with the fantasy
      he knew he'd not lead
for he had a family
      they did not
but he carried the mask
      sincerely wished all
      good luck and cheer
he smiled
swallowed the whiskey
with head bent back
      to cover the tears

highpockets
      we loved ya
      tho we knew not

STORYTELLER

if i were a parent
in today's technology,
at least once a week
i'd pull the plug,
light the room by candles,
and pull my favorite chair
into a corner
i'd gather my children
into a circle
around me,
and tell them stories
of my childhood;
their heritage.

DIBS/NO DIBS

we used to have some wild games
        for sharing
like dibs/no dibs

if you didn't say
        no dibs
before your partner
said dibs
you'd be obligated to share
        your chips,
           cookies, soda
and if you didn't
it was like breaking
        a code of honor
the same stood true
for those who abused
        dibs

our games taught us respect
        humility
           and love
it was cool
        to share
and feel safe
that you would not
be abused

CONVERSATION

Man
I come to you often
....for advice
whether they be problems
....I cannot solve
or directions I should take

but
sometimes I wonder
do you really care
....I mean
you listen well
........don't get me wrong now
........after all
........that's more important
........than talking
............know what I mean
but still
sometimes, just sometimes
I'd like to hear exactly
........what you think
it won't stop me though
from talking to you
........cause I do like
........your listening
and it helps me
to see the bigger scene
get through another day
and for that
........I say thanks
surprised
I finally came to you
for something besides advice
........you know me
sometimes it's hard to express
........feelings
but you know
I truly do love you
and you'll always remain
........my main man
........love ya, bro

Bernard V. Finney, Jr.

is a consultant for Library Development, Department of Education, the State of New York. A long-time resident of Albany, he is looking forward to early retirement so that he can devote full-time to his first love — writing, both poetry and children's stories.

In addition to his own name, Bernard writes poetry as Elizabeth I. Roberts, using both voices "to examine the complexities of human relationships and feelings." He has an affinity for "the outcasts of the world."

I BELIEVE

The world calls me nigger.
    I say I am gentle
    and beautiful.
The night calls me black,
but I have stars burning
    like blue fireflies.
The hate mongers poison my earth,
    and still my flowers
    bloom and release their gifts.
The dream keepers have locked
my ancestors' song in history,
    and still I sing.

The snow hurls its fury at my landscape,
and all things lie beneath white cold.
The suffocation is deep and heavy.
    My seeds, my seeds with hope,
    shall become a resurrection.

There will be Spring.
I believe — in myself!

EXPECTATION

At daybreak, as I stir circles
        in my first cup of coffee,
        I listen to the stillness
            breathing deeply.
        The morning lightens
        as the wind pulls
        a dark blue blanket
            from the sky.

You will soon be here
and our words will fill the room.
        A stone loosens from its shadow
        and a twig snaps.
            You are coming!

I am overjoyed with the expectation
        of talking
        and being heard.

BLACK LEGACY

I want to wrap you in my caring
        give you summer in winter
        grow raspberries in your fertile mind
        and bless your morning with moisture

Let these hands that write poetry
        peel away your night's darkness
        like an onionskin
        no more tears —
        joy shall wet your eyes

I want to wrap you in my warmth
woven from a Black legacy

FROZEN IN THE SNOW

A tomorrow without you
        is without sound
I live in your words
        not in my poetry
Without you
        I am a bird
        frozen in the snow

TEN THOUSAND SPIDERWEBS

The grass and green stillness
        stretch
        to the sky

I discover the dawn
        caught in
        ten thousand spiderwebs

THE SKY BLINKS

The Cardinal clears a song
        from its throat
        as cold wind caresses
        morning's gray plumage

A blossom from a forgotten
        summer floats in circles
        upon the stream
        and quietly sinks
        into the dark tributaries

The sky blinks a snowflake

ANGRY

You were angry
        that love did not conform
        to your specifications
and that swallows chased wind shadows

You are angry still
        but too weak to fight
        as death folds your wings

THE PLAGUE (Aids)

There is silence in the streets
and   in the churches.
The days fall away from the trees.
The dead are shadows passing by.

I am dying from the joy,
that moment,
        long forgotten
in a once sweet summer.
The light has burned out
        in my eyes
and the lesions in my throat choke songs
        I had hoped to sing.

I leave a legacy
        of death
for the unborn.

I cry and waste away,
        by the window
for cure and death are beyond
this room.   The door opens
        slowly;
the shadows hold my hand.

A SUMMER'S AWAKENING

Clouds are pregnant
>with the brooding
>tumultuous thunder
>of a summer's evening.

Raindrops falling from hemlock
>branches make imprints
>upon the silence
>as the forest
>darkness absorbs the rain.

A lonely pond, parched,
>wrinkled and forgotten,
>stirs with excitement.

THE NIGHT

The night sleeps
>and darkness sinks into fields.
I walk along the edge of sounds
>breaking branches
>the wind holding its breath
>>by the creek

To my left is a nest
>soon to be filled with eggs
And then I hear
>the hatching of wet wings
>fanning the morning

The night
>permeates my totality

PROTECT ME

Protect me
>from wolves
>biting at my words

and
>thieves stealing night jewels
>from my heavens

Protect me
>from the hungry
>with their empty bowls

and
>the dying
>clawing at my spirit

TOMORROW IS OUT TO SEA

We do not wait
>for the time to be right
>to give each other
>love,
>laughter
>and rainbows.

We stand at the edges
>of the mist
>listening to
>the sounds of the sea.

We touch!
>Tomorrow is
>far, far
>out to sea

William Goodin

is a single parent of two boys and has involved himself in city politics in St. Louis, Missouri. Caught in the web of "putting it together," his livelihood consists of "whatever I can make happen."

In short, William choses "to title myself a hustler, not so much by decision but because of birth. I pick up the pen in hopes of not picking up the gun. I hope others will grow from my experiences into responsible beings towards humanity; that is the legacy I would like to leave."

I DREAM OF MANY THINGS

I dream
    about escaping the poverty
    that crushes something
        in me —
    about not having to face
        hunger again,
    about not having to sleep
        on the streets.

I dream about love,
    the love I have never known
        personally —
    but the love I am assured
    existed at one time
    among my people.

I dream of revolution,
    not because I promote violence
    but because revolution may be
        necessary
    in order to fulfill
        any of my dreams.

Yes,   I dream of many things —
      of equality for my children —
      of all men living as brothers —
      of dying (if it becomes necessary)
But   beyond all my dreams
      lives one ultimate dream
            — the dream to be free.

IN THE CONFINES OF HIS HOME

Patiently, I watched the man, secretly
watching him not understanding —
></br>but I was,
as I witnessed his unique strategy
    of searching for truths.

Often, he would allow himself to become
    victimized by drugs.
Sometimes, it was his reason to be weak.
Other times, it was for the hell of it.
Sometimes, it was a desire to search
    for the unknown.

He would talk about all the pains
that he had not just lived.
But in talking about his pains,
    he talked about mine.

He would cry silently (filled with pains)
as he read Marcus, King, Douglass, Brooks,
Hughes, Wright, Baldwin
    and all the unknowns
    who have struggled to contribute.
And through their tears, he found comforts
    and inspiration
    to try to make his contribution
    among the known.

He would seat himself.
He would place before him
    a cup of coffee, pencil,
    dictionary, paper
and his magical "weed."
    When he fired up,
    his thoughts would too.

WITHIN MY LIFE

within my life is pains
        eating at my inner self
pains that is frightening
pains that is real
pains that assures me
        urges me to change
yet the reality of my weaknesses
        confronts my manhood
and sometimes I holler
        "I can't "
yet the pain assures me
        I must.

WITH YOU

You came into my life
        with the stolen treasures
        of (maybe) a queen.
Your appearance alone
        struck life back
        into my desolate existence.

With you is an abundance
of knowledge
of   who you are
and   where you are from.
You offer serious suggestions
        for possible solutions
        for our troubled world.

To be with you is forever
        worth the price
of serving you fully — yes,
I claim my rights to be your man,
and   my first duty
        is to protect,
and   with you,
I am stronger than any weapon
men have prepared for war.

With you, my princess,
is always the security
        of me knowing
        who I am.

"ONE NATION UNDER GOD"

In the midst of conversation,
intelligently talking
    about the possibilities
    of bringing social change,
you respond   with leaving.

Yet, constantly at institutions
of reform and education,
you speak about obtaining peace
    between us.
Your exact words:
    "Our nation will not move forward
        if peace is not restored."
Often, we have opportunities
to discuss solutions
as they relate to our peace.
But   you would rather discuss peace
    concerning me
        with someone other than I.
I find that a very sad way,
a very un-for-real way to establish peace
    with me.

You spread rumors about me,
claiming I am racist, I am about violence
because I wear a shirt that says
        . . . REVOLUTION!

You deny me a job
because you justify any wrong
    you know is right
and   you say I lie
when   (you know)
    I speak the truth.

Yes, I talk about revolution,
not always desiring it to come.
In fact, I talk about it
in hopes of us stopping it.
But   you seem content
    with letting it happen,
rather than living peacefully
    as brothers.

LOOKING IN THE MIRROR
(deep memories of a black man)

I sit here staring at myself in the mirror.
        A man half naked to the world.
I tell myself that it isn't me,
        but the mirror differs.
I must challenge the opposition.

Who am I? Am I not a creature of uniqueness
        Have I not been blessed
        with this opportunity to live?
Often, I ask myself — for what reason
should I not advance my being into my dreams?
        Have I not a heart?
For what reason should mine be torn apart?
For what reason is my soul on fire?

Have I that right . . . . . to let injustices
destroy not only myself but, indeed, my race?
Do I not owe myself the opportunity to be free?
Have I not the right to search life
        while looking for me?
I look at myself in the mirror.
        I see a man oppressed.
        I see emptiness in my eyes.
        I see pain in my face.
Why have I not the right
to be part of advancing humanity?
My independence would reward my race.

My soul bothers me with consistency.
Often I tell myself my heart is gone.
        But it is not.
To not bow down to oppression is a glory.
        (A mission must have a completion.)
Have I not a name and identity?

Within the realities of struggling for freedom
        lies a contradiction.
Of course, I have learned to think
in terms of working contradictions out.
So I try.   What else have I?
Have I not spoken the truth?
For what reason is injustice right?

FORGIVE ME FOR CRYING BUT I CAN'T HELP IT

yes, i cry   i cry for many reasons
one reason is that i cry because you won't

i cry   i hate leaving the people i love
while going on ventures with others
    that is part of our bondagement
    but it's necessary . . .
yes, i cry because i can't make you understand

i cry for my brother henry
he died such a young vicious life
    shot in the head while at home
i cry not only because he died
but because it shouldn't have been like that
    i cry because of my brother donnie
who became addicted to drugs
as he fought trying to become free
    i cry for my brother lavon
who has become dissolute and contented
for no reason 'cept   confusement

yes, i cry   i cry for me
knowing that my body and mind
    have been enraged with hate
struggling and fighting trying to get free

i cry for my sisters trapped in the stinks
and corruptions   of the ghetto
i cry for my sons who are six and five
who have to grow up fighting
    confusement from the start

yep . . . damn right i cry
i cry because i don't understand why
        you don't
i cry because i hate to leave
i cry because tomorrow i may die

forgive me for crying   but i can't help it
    i cry because it may be
    i have to start the revolution

Albert McClure

is a University of Minnesota graduate and has retired after 30 years as a Northwest Airlines employee. A lifelong resident of Minneapolis, he enjoys traveling with his wife and spending time with his grandchildren.

A contributor to numerous poetry anthologies, Albert writes to "create a record of myself, with all of the nuances that entails, and to leave a legacy." His special interest is "the complexity of male/female relationships."

WHY DO I WEEP?

Why do I weep?
I weep for thee
for the world you want
will never be —
a world filled
with peace and love.
That's why I weep.
I weep for thee.

Why do I weep?
I weep for me
for I could never
be to thee
a shelter
in a storm-tossed sea
of hatred, of bigotry.
That's why I weep.
I weep for me.

Why do I weep?
I weep for mankind
that can conquer space
but still is blind
to one another.
That's why I weep.
I weep for them.

Why do I weep?
I weep for thee
I weep for them
I weep for me
and the bells toll.

THE WIND OF DEATH

The wild wind is blowing
Gathering speed as it cuts
Across the empty plain,
Killing everything it touches
With its icy hand.
       The Indians call it —
       The Wind of Death!

The swirling snow
Sifts through cracks
Of the cabin door,
Leaving a trail of ghostly footprints
Across the barren floor.

A frightened child,
Huddling under a buffalo robe,
Crouches in a corner.

It's been years
Since I thought of that cabin
And the frightened toddler
Of my childhood.
But now, deep inside of me,
I sense that wild wind blowing,
Gathering speed as it slowly moves
Across this empty plain.
       The Indians call it —
       The Wind of Death!

THE SHE-HUNTERS OF THE DEEP FOREST

In the evening when the young men gather
around the campfire to listen to the elders,
the wisemen often speak softly and reverently
of the She-Hunters of the Deep Forest:
      "Beware, for she is elusive,
          cunning and dangerous.
      Should you meet one,
      do not lie with her.
      She will cast her magic spell,
      and you will be her slave forever."

I did not believe the wisemen until, by chance,
I met a She-Hunter of the Deep Forest.
She was elusive, comely and willing.
      I lay with her,
and   she cast her magic spell.

At first light of dawn, she was gone,
silently disappearing into the fading night,
leaving behind on my bed of leaves
a faint musky order to remind me of her —
          of that night.

I never saw her again,
although I've looked everywhere.
      Still, I cannot forget her —
The eyes of a startled deer are her eyes;
the murmur of the brook is her voice;
the wind rustling in tall grass
is the rustling of her skirt;
the elusive dark shadows of the deep forest
          remind me of her.

I wish I had heeded the warning of the elders.

OLD PEOPLE

I think I know
why old people
huddle in the sun,
ever grateful
for its warmth.

They are lonesome
for the warmth of friends,
companions and the love
that once warmed their lives.
Now, only the hot rays
of the sun engulf them,
its warmth a gentle reminder
of what was long ago.

AFRICA

Night cover my eyes
Immerse me in your blackness
Blot out the day — the whiteness of reality
Let the ghosts, the voices of my ancestors
       merge into my consciousness
Let the warring elements of my blood fuse
Let me drift in your fetal blackness
And absorb my blackness — my heritage.

Nubian as the night is your blackness
And the tears that flow
       are for the expatriates
       who by their very existence
       lose their negritude — their blackness

Oh Africa, embrace me like the night
       embraces me.

VALUES

In a world of low values
I place high value on this
        love of mine.
It can't be bought, traded or sold.
It can only be given —
And I give it freely
        to you.

A PART OF LIVING

A part of living is giving,
        giving of oneself —
        freely, fully, deeply,
        without reservation,
        without guilt.

A part of living is receiving,
        freely, fully, deeply
        without reservation,
        without guilt.

A part of living is loving;
for then the circle is complete;
for then all parts of the circle meet.

    For living   is giving
                          and receiving
                          and loving.

FASCINATING

You are fascinating —
not because of your beauty
but because of your aura
        of promises.
Promises hint
from every salient part of you,
        promise of fulfillment.
(I am under your spell.)

NOTHINGNESS OF SILENCE

The nothingness of silence
assails my ears
        makes my senses reel
         I am disoriented

Before I heard
waves of sound
            people talking
            the roar of traffic
            wailing ghetto boxes
            the hum of the city
Now the nothingness of silence
fills my ears
        and I fear what I cannot hear

Now I   wake to silence
        walk to silence
        think to silence

There are so many things
I still   want to hear from you
         want to share with you
             the nuances of pillowtalk
             the intimacy of your whisper

I am adapting
But, it's like walking
        to a stumbling beat

The nothingness of silence
fills my ears
        and I fear
        what I cannot hear

Dr. Gary Smith

teaches in the English Department of Southern Illinois University-Carbondale, has published poems in a number of literary magazines and authored two volumes of poetry. He also co-edited a volume of critical essays on Gwendolyn Brooks and edited another on Melvin B. Tolson.

On poetry, he agrees with W.H. Auden that it makes little or nothing happen. He writes essentially in order to freshen our language and perspective on ageless human problems.

SECONDHAND RADIO

The Christmas my grandfather bought
a secondhand radio from a white farmer
he sometimes worked for during winter,
the cardboard box in which it was kept
sat untouched on the kitchen table.

He had promised it as a Christmas gift,
but forbade everyone but my grandmother
to turn it on.
                    Devil's work! he said,
whenever one of his children asked
why the box was forbidden — even though
it had been promised the year before.

White folks done found a way to talk
to us without being in the same room,
he explained, while peering at the box,
could be a sign of much worse to come,
some sign of worse, much worse to come.

MOSE GOODMAN

    Mose Goodman was the oldest black in Holly Springs.
A burly man, coffee-brown in color, with arms
that hung from his body like cords of knotted rope.

    Some said he had been among the first slaves
brought to this country from Africa.
    Others said
he had been neither an African nor a slave.

    They said he appeared one winter morning
dressed in a sleeveless overcoat and straw hat.
    He wandered the backroads of Holly Springs,
indifferent to the wind that tore at his hat
and the rain that soaked his overcoat.
    At each farmhouse he visited, they gave
him whatever was left on the dinnertable
and listened as he told of things he had seen:
> "you see, nothing come of itself.
> Something belong to another something
> and that something belong
> to something else.
>
> Now, as I sees it, someone got the 'some' right
> but they got the 'thing' wrong.
> Some got more and other folk got less —
> black and white —
> as I sees it."

    Then after Mose had filled himself with dinner scraps,
he left, and they again questioned his origins.
    What they all knew — without knowing why —
was that Mose Goodman did not belong to Holly Springs,
and his straw hat and overcoat did not belong to winter.

WINTERS IN HOLLY SPRINGS

Winters in Holly Springs were stillborn:
        lean, amphibious creatures that crawled
        upon the sun-scorched earth, copulated,
        bore their young and died — in the time
        when the once-green fields mildewed.

Blacks called it the season of trust.
        They would make the twice-yearly trip
        to settle accounts with merchants,
        who had loaned them seed and tools
        with which to make the land fruitful.

My grandfather usually went alone,
        dressed in his Sunday coat and hat,
        seated on the buckboard of his mulewagon —
        with a look of polished conviction about
        what he owed and intended to pay.

He took along his list of groceries
        that were needed to tide his family over,
        during the time the land was barren.
He promised to bring
        shoes and candy for the young
        who ran after the wagon.

The children then, heard the wagon
when grandfather returned from Macon:
        The sharp clacks of the wooden wheels
        pulled by the heavy-breathing mules.
Everyone else knew he had nothing.

SLAVERY MADE YOU A POET
(for Phyllis Wheatley 1753-1784)

Slavery made you a poet — not religion!
Despite Jefferson, democracy's aristocrat,
who only saw the cloak of your race —
not his own ambivalence about slavery.

For those who still question your art,
let them count the many who neither saw
nor imagined a life apart from bondage;
who, if they lacked courage, had conviction
to smother oppression with blameless praise!

But you, Phyllis, neither slave nor free,
were an enigma for Tories and Wigs alike.
You found your gift in well-placed rhymes;
a painted bird that eluded its captors
and gave mockery a cutting new name.

YOUR POEM TO PHYLLIS
(for Jupiter Hammond 1711-1806)

Your poem to Phyllis, hardly a poem,
born of desire to touch another
who, like you, had heeded the Revival;
or followed the Pilgrims whose faith
was tempered by suffering — but whose
suffering was tempered by slavery.

Two caged larks, trained in song,
your bright, African plumage wilted
in the frigid New England climate;
and the sense too, of longing blunted
by patience which holds its breath.

Yet envious, still wondrous of how
poor Phyllis had managed her bondage,
you wrote to ask if her soul was saved.

UNFINISHED ERRANDS
(for Robert E. Hayden 1913-1980)

Unfinished errands blacken my hands
like burnt cork the minstrel's face.
The harried postman's crepe soled shoes
trample tender snails to earthworms.

And you, Hayden, accounts settled,
your thick bottomed glasses sucked
against your eyes which scuttled
across the illuminated page like paramecia.

All for naught,
                you might've said,
then turned the other cheek to show
its twin, too, stung scarlet-blue
by the leather hand of misfortune.

First your father's adopted son;
later the world's adopted poet.

THE WINTER OF YOUR DEATH
(for Jupiter Hammond 1711-1806)

The winter of your death, I imagine
you wandering past the sea-scoured
coastline of Lloyd's Estate.
        Utterly lost,
alone, barely free of the receding, blue horizon.

Your incessant quarrel with God over;
yet the leg-iron you wore like a mantle
still fastened you to one place, one time.

What miracles did you expect there —
the Red Sea's parting at Moses' command;
or Jonah's descent into the whale's belly?

Surely not this quiet leave-taking —
one man pitted against the ungodly,
and psalms you could vaguely recall.

THE FATE OF AN INNOCENT DOG
(for George Moses Horton 1797-1883)

An innocent dog is not entirely unlike
his Master.
                Both are tied to destiny's
chain, though each claims a different fate.

No matter, here, that one is black —
                the other white;
that one is taught to heel and beg,
while the other urges him on;
or, alas, that the imaginary chain —
                link by link —
is circuitous reasons joined by lies.

One stands convinced of his direction;
but needs the other to pull along.

Thus, George Moses Horton, a slave
of circumstances beyond his control,
trots after his Master's command;
yet, by art, stakes his mortal claim.

FLANNEL SUIT

    My grandfather died twice before he was dead.

    The first time, he lay in the rubble of his spirit,
his head sunk between two pillows, and his silences
punctuated with snatches of hymns and prayers.

    The second time, he rose late one night,
dressed himself in his good flannel suit
and walked towards what was soon to be morning.

Chema Ude

was born in the Igbo-speaking state in eastern Nigeria, the eldest of six children. He moved to southern California in 1970 as a refugee of the Biafran war.

The holder of a masters degree in Urban Planning and Public Administration, he works as a senior city-planner and currently lives in Riverside, California. In addition to poetry, he writes fiction and feature articles and enjoys photography, tennis, raquetball and work.

SAVED AFRICA

Here, admidst the squalid village huts
where rats are tolerated guests
that nightly gnaw at sleeper's soles
just to stay alive;

Here where babies die
more often than they are born
and rash-ridden toddlers
are pregnant with kwashiorkor;

It is here that the white man's churches
sit lofty, fat and clean
with foreign stained glasses of white
        Christs
and offering plates of gilded silver
into which every week and twice on
        Sundays
pious sheep of the Savior's flocks
are milked and bled
till our bones are bare
suffering our bodies
to save our souls,

                thank God.

A CAPITAL PRAYER

Enter my life, O Lord,
buy me another Cadillac.
Guide my humble tottering steps,
    Dear God,
may my insurance premiums be paid.

Almighty King of kings,
may Uncle Sam reign
globally supreme forevermore
    above Buddhist monks
    and Islamic Commies.
May thy will be done,
              Amen.

AFRICAN PATRICIDAL PLOT

These wealths are ours they stealthily stash
from the coffers of their rigged care.
It is bad enough they steal their charge,
they salt the hurt and flaunt their dash;

ten percent we know is their going rate.
Swiss accounts and jets with turbocharge
make conversations in high circles.
We are the slaves of greedy leaders.

We watched them fend off bigger foes;
now they themselves are the evil hands
that grasp a leeching hold on our hearts
we must amputate to free our gangrened lands.

For the sake of our future children
we will unshackle and rename for us
our own dear priceless worth
for freedom and justice we hunger.

HIDEBOUND

the cause is skin-deep
they love the land
       they pain to keep
their very own nativeland
what else is there to do?

they sweat-soak the diamond and gold
       to glitter
that stocks bull markets
and chokers the necks and wrists
of men and women
in lofty anticeptic places;
       places where escargot
drowned with chateau blanc
insulates exploitive consciences
from human corrals in Transvaal
       shantytowns of
           Basutoland and Johannesburg

they love the land
       they try to own
held in stagnant foreign hands
their very own fatherland
as omnipotent Tixo watches on
and the titihoyas chorus their
       larkish indifferent freedom lullabies
what else is there to do?

until the velds are set ablaze
with scarlet rivers of crushed lilies drowned
and cleansed in frenzied joyous feasts
to end their long denied uhuru victory
       for their motherland

whatever else
is there to do?

MY NIGERIAN FREEDOM

When I was growing up at home
> we learned

twinkle twinkle stars
all in foreign english
God washed our sins
white as white man's snow
P.W.D. men
> hauled trash
> mended our roads

and the street corner pumps
flowed rusty or with twitching things
> but often flowed.

The power that storms took
returned when the rains stopped.
We hurt all over
from foreign dominance.

But now our turn has come
now we are free
free to fly our own freedom kite
which replaces the union jack
our own national anthem
fills our hearts with pride
> "Nigeria we hail thee
> our own dear native land..."

our time has come
we are free
free at long last
> "...to serve our sovereign
> motherland"

But soon
the pipes run dry
and power lines are too weak
> even for vulture perch

Our curtains are now wrought iron steel
with triple Union locks
of deadbolt shafts
that thieves defy.

> I wish dear God
> I was growing up again
> complaining but contented.

NATURE'S WAY

It didn't matter anyway
that Dinosaurus Rex
lost pace with time
       and died

It doesn't matter anyway
that the Dodo
       was a bird

It won't matter anyway
that polluted man
       lived
then destroyed himself
       in an atomic puff

Nature rights itself
       always

THE ONE I CHOSE
(from a lady in pain)

We pulled dandelions
from your lawn
they are gone now
but we left the roots

I am the bluegrass we played on
mauled trampled and bruised
in agony of the violence
of your love charade

I am the ardent prize-fighter
you are the casanova that I won
I am the loser

The weeds of your life
left dormant seeds
I now water
with my bleeding heart

OUR AFRICAN PARENTS

For what is there for them
to live?
The chain of our lineage is snapped
at the strongest link.
    We their hope
    have all gone away
    to dazzle towns
    to become modern.

As mutual reluctant burdens
    we and our parents
are dying species
dis   orien   ted
out of rhyme
    seeking our
    enlightening dawn
    westward.

MANHOOD RIGHTS

Oh well, they said I must bury him
Christian
Without guns, goat blood
And raw white hen with its head
    twisted off
And ekpe masquerade
To call him home as the real man
That we still know

They said I must be the man
That my father would want
For a son, to walk his own steps

I could not shed this one good tear
To speak my love, unrestrained
Even to his cold reasoning ears

Right now I want to be a woman
My sisters wail their catharsis
Instead, I taste the blood inside my lips
From the yoke of manhood rites

The chief, the pastor, the village
Everyone watching
    a strong brave man
Their own son

Ken Wibecan

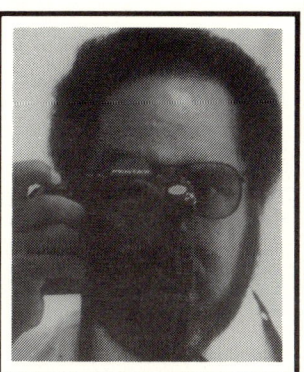

lives in a Southern California Black community, has a Liberal Arts degree from Goddard College in Vermont. A former news colmnist and community college instructor, he now writes full time for a living.

In his poetry, Ken searches for what he calls "inconsistencies," like the preacher who talks but doesn't practice, or paradoxes like why the black community is the most religious and also has the most crime. "It is not hard to find inconsistencies — they are everywhere, even in this brief bio."

BLACK HISTORY

Like an empty vessel
they filled me
with past lives
black empires
at Mali and Songhai
5000 years of civilization
constructed with black hands

> adam and eve
> were black they said
> like your momma

i right on took it all in
but they drove off
in a black mercedes
before i could find out
what we had done
for we   lately

TO BLACK WOMAN

when i first made love to you
many whitewashed years ago
i did not know you
my mind had been polluted
with power's sewage

you did not smile at me
from cigarette ads
or seduce me
into cadillacs and color tvs
your eyes did not seek mine
in darkened movie theatres
it was liztaylormarilynmonroe
and a cast of white thousands
(you furnished the comic relief)

i learned to ignore you
seeking beauty elsewhere
but beauty was defined by others
and i was left with nostrils filled
with the stench of burning hair
and greasy-cheeked mementoes of your affection
conk was king and we mere slaves
to our golden dreams

then the darkness of malcolm came
and my eyes were able to see
that what i had rejected in you
i despised in me

now your dark thighs sing to me
of past glories from africa's womb
zulu kings ashanti warriors
      egyptian empires
becoming clearer in memory's eye

heritage denied now fills
the vacuum of my soul
and i a man once more
can take my place
on the lists of time
powerful and strong
not to be denied

EARTHBOUND

I'm tired of writing about black.

I'd rather write about the outdoors
far from the smog and scurry of civilization
    where, on a moonless night,
      the stars float down
like a giant bowl-full
had been inverted over my head;
    where, on sunny mornings
I can strap on my cross-country skies
and make new tracks through fresh snow
    in the silent woods.

I want to dream
about kings, queens, castles
and fanciful creatures in colorful worlds
    where adventure is everyday,
where spaceships ply the skies
and wondrous creatures with two heads,
tentacles and several pairs of arms
    are my best friends.

I want to write poems
that make people laugh,
smile, remember
and sometimes cry,
    or stories
about my old dog, Pepe,
and fictional tales
for everyone's children
    to enjoy.

But it is not yet time to fly —
    I am earthbound
    I am black.

HAROLD

tall/black/ambitious
followed all the rules
BA/economics
MA/american business
hard work

thought about business
most of the time
loved his family
feared god
opposed gun control
voted republican

only "knee-grow" on the block
white folks invited him
to parties golf matches
afternoon teas

> (tacitly he understood
> his son was not to date
> their daughters)

speeding through orange county
(they said) two white policemen
called him "boy" and "nigger"
for the first time ever

the next day
found him dangling
in the garage   rope
efficiently knotted
behind his neck
dried tear tracks
trailing down
his swollen black face

all he had wanted was to be
    an american

RETURN ENGAGEMENT

the girls i loved
           and lost   and left
stand there still
waiting for my kiss

they remain as before
           breasts firm   and pointed
eyes wide
with wonder

it is i who has turned
           grown jaded   with experience
the veneer of youth
eroded by time

but still ready
           at a moment's notice
to summon them back
for a return engagement
                          while i sleep

ADVENTURE

In the space of three days
they climbed Mount Everest,
laughed at a hurricane;
their tears of joy
combined with the torrent
to create a mighty river.

They canoed far into the past,
discovered the Pyramids
ancient temples
to the Goddess of Love.

Barehanded
he rescued her
from three alligators
one fire-breathing dragon.

They made love at twilight
and gave birth to the moon.

Then they parted
because black
was not in style
in Minneapolis that year.

WHY DOGS BARK AT NIGHT

swift-legged couriers
of instinct
and timeless memory
prowl the dark

pupils distended
hackles raised
they search
the corridors of night

and bark
their warnings
of ancient terrors
that we have not yet
learned to see

PHOTOGRAPH OF A 1923 LYNCHING

Fly covered black body
dangling from a tree
while long shadow fingers
of evening sun entertain
with bloody light shows.

Grotesque darky/scarecrow,
fruit of white love,
life plucked from him
by goodcitizens anonymous
in their converted bed sheets.

Wives and children
look on, observe, dig it.
Picnic lunches almost gone.
Drinking wine, lemonade, mint juleps,
happy smiles flush
their fishbelly redneck faces.

"Shake the tree again, Daddy,
I want to see him dance."

Things were simple then:
one nigger equaled one picnic.
But technology has advanced with time.
White folks are more sophisticated now
. . . and bed sheets come in colors.

Gene A. Williams

also writes and performs his poetry under the name Sunji Ali and is a junior high school teacher in "a tough part" of Los Angeles. He grew up in the San Francisco/Oakland Bay area and earned a masters degree in African History from UCLA.

Active in International Black Writers and Artists, Inc., he is the leader of the "Soul Vision Poetry Workshop" and is involved in a "personal search for meaning living in a predominantly white society and being treated as a second-class citizen."

POETRY IN THE ALLEY

This love poem, brothers,
>was born in an alley
>behind a beautiful store.
And people always keep coming,
>coming back for more.
This poem has love in it,
honey all around — sugar singing
through it (though some people say
>there is nothing to it).

A woman named Sally came by
>for a stay
and wrote a poem
while singing in the alley.

Poetry must be like love juices,
>must flow —
and poor people must know
where to go to get help.
The people-walkers are lonely,
>none are free.
But poetry must be
>in the alley
behind all the beautiful stores.

In the dark, sweetness of night,
love (poetry) must come to light.

THE BLUES IS SWEET WATER

The blues is sweet water
coming from dark water, back water

Blues came up before
        sunrise
was in cotton sacks
(between short naps and quick snaps)
        in between long dreams
                that could only die

Cotton was cold, the boll weevil
        a relentless evil
Shanty towns sprang up around
        mill towns
Lumberjacks died in their sleep
Yet   melodies became sweet
        harmonious sound
You could hear Mississippi John Hurt
        for miles around

Blues took root
        in the Black rivers
        of the Old South
It was in the water
that made jazz a river,
spirituals swing,
the back beat in Coltrane's
        "My Favorite Things" . . .

When Reconstruction died
        poor people cried
        the ballot box closed
Then Blues began to roll
like   dark water, sweet water
        going for a stroll . . .
Back water, sweet water rising up.
Bessie Smith and Brownie McGhee
        longing to be free . . .

WALKING ON THE WATER

There is a water-spring
        in my vision
of man;   the eternal
water springs   and sings,
brings   much
        needed rain;
There is water in my vision
        of the sky;
        I don't ask why
the sky brings rain
        out of the blue
(I leave those things, dear
rainbow,   up to you.)

Most men walk on water
        when it rains;
they see little bits of blue
in everything rosy or red;
we wash our clothes in the rain
        seek laughter over pain . . .

And why do water-birds
        fly   away?
Why   do they play?

And what does Spring water
have to do with my vision of man?
What does fire have to do
        with virgin land?
What do flames have
        to do with burnt-out names
        before Spring water
        makes for fertile plains?

A water spring makes
        the youth in me sing
        the water from the sky
to bring   fresh rain
when day and night
never seem the same;
        a walk on water
        is not a real thing,
yet —   all the world's flowers
speak   gentle of spring . . .

HAZEL EYES
(for Hazel Clayton Harrison)

Jazz is a copper-colored sky,
      an evening-eyed,
luscious, lavender woman.

A river is a thousand lakes
      laughing by my backdoor;
and soft eyes see through
the evening sunset of the blues.

Have you ever been close
      when a black woman cries?
Heard the blues of Billie's bounce
happy feet, walking, dancing
with warm, soul-soft eyes?

Hear "Willow Weep For Me"
Embrace "Embraceable You"
Get into "Jug" eyes
Get off on "Every Day I Have The Blues"
Taste the silk of Duke's "Satin Doll"

Blue skies reign well past midnight
      and get into "Hazel Eyes"
till you feel the morning sun
      coming through
and   forget the lonely night,
      and lonely you
and   the dark, dreary day
when you had nothing to lose
      but the blues
and   didn't have to worry
about buying a new pair of shoes . . .

MOTHER DIDN'T TELL ME TO CRY
(but to fight back)

Mother didn't tell me to cry
        no, never
She didn't tell me to sit back
and pout about nothing,
to sit in the back of the bus
        and think about "them" and "us."

She didn't tell me to cry
        but to fight back
with words —
weapons that mean something:
        To burn some midnight oil,
        Carry my books all the way home;
To deal with some math
and chemistry and all the earth,
biological and physical sciences,
        history and humane letters.

She told me to read the "psalms"
of   James Baldwin,
Ralph Ellison,   and Richard Wright
        To study all the wrongs
        that parade as rights

To make sense of "Daylight Saving Time"
and "Monk Time,"   "Coltrane Time"
        and all the "Bad Times"
        that make strong men sing.

Mother didn't tell me to cry
        but to fight back
with   the weapons of peace,
        the words of war,
the songs
        that savor the meanings
        and moods
        and   an ancient solitude.

POETRY AND SONG
(rising to the moment)

When the wine flows gentle
out of rare old kegs
and the power of a hot July
flows into an August autumn,

And the poet rises to the moment
losing his edge of despair
making merry in the midst of senseless shame
taking pieces of night
and   making days full,
pieces of a man
and   making him whole,

And the wine flows gently
not only in the spring
but whenever men freely choose to sing
ballads or blues songs
of night, of paradise,
of nothingness amplified.

The poet rises to the moment
and   makes sweet
           memories come alive —
the fourth of July battle
or   Orange and Roses;
and William Grant Still's long silence
           continues to speak

The golden moments when he sang
           Mozart in the spring
and   Chopin in September;
The poet speaks through songs
and   does remember
           the rhymes that speak
of rivers in the sand
Golden mornings that make matter moist
and   modern man . . . golden.